I

TRUST

AUDREY KINEARD

DEDICATION

To my Family:

My mother Elder Pearline Hammett- McFadden for introducing me to "Jesus Christ" and instilling in me to "Trust" God.

To Freddie my husband, my children Brittney, Freddie Louis and Bridgett. You are important to me and without your support this would have been difficult. But your love and support make it easy. Love you all

Thank you for believing in me.

Contents

ACKNOWLEDGEMENTS

I would like to express my appreciation to my wonderful friend Rev. Joe W. Rucker for his support and encouraging words of wisdom. Rev. JWR, your weekly talks and numerous deadlines, get me here. Thanks, my brother! Thank you, Sharelle Fung-a-wing, for the audio set-up. Thank you to the Victory International Praise and Worship Center congregation for their support.

I love my family, Margie, Christina, Robertha, Thelma, Elias, Fred G., Vernon, Estelle, and Calvin for your support and motivation. Mrs. Pearline mom, you always believed and encouraged me to aim high.

My loving husband Freddie, children Brittney and Freddie Louis thanks for everything, such as your ideas, jokes and long days. A big thanks to daughter Bridgett for her creative and artistic cover and other design.

Thank you to my spiritual family, Apostle Shelia Johnson, Min. Brenda Fite , Pastor Diana Hugger and Pastor Jerry Jones for praying for me.

Ultimately, my greatest gratitude belongs to the Lord. God gave me this passion and I am very grateful to him. All the Glory belongs to GOD.

DAY ONE

Habakkuk 2:2

*Then the Lord said to me, "Write my answer
plainly on tablets, so that a runner can carry
the correct message to others.*

T his vision is for the future. It describes the end, and it will be fulfilled. If it seems slow in coming, wait patiently, for it will surely take place. It will not be delayed. While you wait, stay focus and look at it. " The Vision"

DAY TWO

Ephesians 3:20-21 TLB

*Now glory be to God, who by his mighty power
at work within us is able to do far more than we
would ever dare to ask or even dream of-
infinitely beyond our highest prayers, desires,
thoughts, or hopes. May he be given glory
forever and ever through endless ages because
of his master plan of salvation for the Church
through Jesus Christ.*

When you feel like giving up. Know that God is in control. God plans for my life is always better. God has granted us with power to do the impossible. As I began to walk in God's plan, the enemy tried to steal my focus. When I focused on my strength, I lose focus on God. I had to look beyond my past failures. Don't let your past failures derail your future. I had to let God lead the way. Remember, God gets the Glory when battles are won. What's your battle? Have you tried my God? My God is a great defender.

DAY THREE

Romans 3:3-4 TLB

True, some of them were unfaithful, but just because they broke their promises to God, does that mean God will break his promises? Of course not! Though everyone else in the world is a liar, God is not. Do you remember what the book of Psalms says about this? That God's words will always prove true and right, no matter who questions them.

God cannot lie. Your future is already written in the earth as it is in heaven. God keeps his word according to his promise for you. You must live by Faith. Obey God's word and move in the direction that God has ordained for your life. I had to focus on God. Everyday with the Lord is sweeter than the day before. You could hold God to his word and never forget who he is in your life.

DAY FOUR

1 Corinthians 2:9 NIV

However, as it is written: "What no eye has seen, what no ear has heard, and what no human mind has conceived" ---the things God has prepared for those who love him---

God sees our future beyond what we see. Our natural eyes can't see what's in the supernatural. God has already whispered your future into the atmosphere. How could you see unlimited possibilities, if your mind is blocked? Trusting God requires you not to reason with yourself. Remember newton's law unless you stop it, the motion will continue. Allow the word of God to be in motion in your life. It will take you places you could only IMAGINE.

DAY FIVE

Numbers 23:19 NIV

God is not human, that he should lie, not a human being, that he should change his mind. Does he speak and then not act? Does he promise and not fulfill?

God word is true. He will finish what he has started. When God give you a word of revelation, you must follow his plan and understand his timing is not your timing. The word of God is true and active. The word of God has a start and a completion date in mind for you. His grace is sufficient. According to the word of God, whatever God started in you, He will finish. (Roman 8:28) If you will continue to follow him. He will complete the process. Can I get an "AMEN"! I am a witness.

DAY SIX

Jeremiah 29:11 NIV

For I know the plans I have for you," declares the Lord, "plans to prosper you and not to harm you, plans to give you hope and a future.

W ho could better set you up for a bright bless future beside the one who created everything? God's blueprint for me had stop signs, warnings, peaks and lows. God wrote victories in certain areas, where my faith was tested and passed. Since God is the master creator, his plan was an "A" plan. He did not need my help. But you know I had my plan "B" ("B" plan - Behind God's Plan). God plan was for me to Prosper (resources), Hope (don't get weary) and a promising Future (already spoken). But my plan "B" only delayed what was already in motion. The Enteral God always got 'A" perfect plan. His plan cannot fail.

DAY SEVEN

John 1:1 NIV

In the beginning was the Word, and the Word was with God, and the Word was God.

God is the creator of all. As I began to embrace what God gave me. I often wonder if God really had all this for me. Never underestimate how great is our God in regards of your insecurities. God wants to give us his very best. He has already spoken words of "greatness" over our lives in the beginning. My name was written at the beginning of the storylines. It is my time.

DAY EIGHT

Philippians 3:14 NIV,

*I press on toward the goal to win the
prize for which God has called me
heavenward in Christ Jesus.*

I love this scripture. It lets me know, it takes patience and endurance to be successful. This race requires you to stay focus on the reward, the prize to which God has promise you. The "press" is your obedience to God's word. Let your trust in God connect you to your promise. Say with me "I Press". Alright, let's go, let's go get it and let's watch God perform.

DAY NINE

Romans 8:28

And we know that in all things God works for the good of those who love him, who[i have been called according to his purpose.

What do you do, when God speak a word to YOU? It means he knows you. You must have a relationship with him. Your past mistakes have not and will not keep you from obtaining the good things God has for you. You are chosen. I am chosen. So, what are you waiting on? The process has already been worked-out for you. "Just go and do it!" All things work together for the Good. You got the hook-up!

DAY TEN

Proverbs 3:5-6 AMPC

*Lean on, trust in, and be confident in the Lord
with all your heart and mind and do not rely
on your own insight or understanding. In all
your ways know, recognize, and
acknowledge Him, and He will direct and
make straight and plain your paths.*

OK drop the Mic. A powerful scripture. Everyday, I had to go to work, I had to stand in the face of those who I knew dislike me. They would do anything to sabotage my career. But I had to press, pray, and to stay one step ahead of the enemy to accomplish my goals. I could not allow them to see me sweat. Yeah, I had to trust the process. If there's no process, there's no progress. So, I understood that had to Ask God for a strategic plan to defeat the opposition. I needed "grace knowledge" and God's strategy to keep it together.

DAY ELEVEN

1 John 4:8 NLT

*But anyone who does not love does not know
God, for God is love.*

Gdo is love. God's love speaks loudly to and through his believers. Show love everywhere you go, to those you meet is an opportunity to share love, and to embrace love. As believers, we must show the world Love. I know in life we feel that love cannot be extended to everyone. But since we know God is love and God abides in us. Then we are capable to Love. Try it through God's grace.

DAY TWELVE

James 1:2-4 NIV

*Consider it pure joy, my brothers and sisters,
whenever you face trials of many
kinds, because you know that the testing of
your faith produces perseverance. Let
perseverance finish its work so that you may
be mature and complete, not lacking
anything.*

How do you response during a crisis? By FAITH. This is when your Faith power evolves. Use your FAITH Power. Have the God kind of Faith. Consider it pure joy. I know I can do all things with Faith power. Remember there is no new temptation to God. He will bring you out. I'm a "witness".

F-aith

A-lways

I-nvolves

T-rusting

H-im

DAY THIRTEEN

Psalm 55:22 AMPC

Cast your burden on the Lord releasing the weight of it and He will sustain you; He will never allow the consistently righteous to be moved (made to slip, fall, or fail).

Finally, I did it! I released my daily frustrations and struggles to God. It's not easy. I thought I was able to handle and fix it. I said to myself, I 'll do it, Audrey's way. Boy was I wrong. Things went from bad to worse. I'm a work in progress, I'm still learning, still growing and improving daily. Caution! "remodeling in progress". So, my advice to you; pray about it, then give it totally to God and think no more about it. Tell God I can't carry this anymore, fix it. Then, I thanked him in advance. So, try it. Throw it to him, NOW!

DAY FOURTEEN

1 Peter 5:8 AMPC

*Be well balanced (temperate, sober of mind),
be vigilant and cautious at all times; for that
enemy of yours, the devil, roams around like
a lion roaring in fierce hunger, seeking
someone to seize upon and devour.*

<hr/>

Meditate daily on the word of God is my first rule of balance. When you and your spirit are ONE, then, you are in a healthy spiritual place. Learn to listen to self, the inner you. A healthy inner spirit is necessary for a well-balance spiritual person.

DAY FIFTEEN

Psalm 1:3 AMPC

*And he shall be like a tree firmly planted and
tended by the streams of water, ready to
bring forth its fruit in its season; its leaf also
shall not fade or wither; and everything he
does shall prosper and come to maturity.*

Your timing isn't Gods timing. Timing is everything. (Ecclesiastes 3:1) You must be firmly planted (your understanding & obedience) in the word of God. Understand your place in this universe. God created you for a purpose. Find your passion then ask and seek God for guidance to bring it to manifestation. God's timing will reveal your success.

DAY SIXTEEN

James 4:2 NIV

*You want what you don't have, so you
scheme and kill to get it. You are jealous of
what others have, but you can't get it, so you
fight and wage war to take it away from
them. Yet you don't have what you want
because you don't ask God for it.*

It's Simple. Our God is a giving God. He is waiting for his children to Ask. Do you have a burning desire? Seek God first and he is the rewarder. So, Ask, Seek and Knock. Because if you ask, it is given, if you seek, you will find and if you knock it will be open. (Matthew 7:24-27) ASK God!

DAY SEVENTEEN

Psalm 18:21 AMPC

For I have kept the ways of the Lord and
have not wickedly departed from my God.

There were times in my life, when I questioned my walk with God. I noticed that everyone around me were receiving blessing. I was seeking God but there was no manifestation in my life. Then, I realized that I had to stay focus, stay on course and stay committed to God. Don't try to get even. This walk of life required me to be discipline and firmly planted in the word of God. I know that I am precious in God's eyesight. He called me his daughter. Therefore, nothing shall be impossible.

DAY EIGHTEEN

Isaiah 54:17 AMPC

But no weapon that is formed against you shall prosper, and every tongue that shall rise against you in judgment you shall show to be in the wrong. This peace, righteousness, security, triumph over opposition is the heritage of the servants of the Lord those in whom the ideal Servant of the Lord is reproduced; this is the righteousness or the vindication which they obtain from Me this is that which I impart to them as their justification, says the Lord.

P rayer is the KEY! It's not just about saying a few scriptures and saying Amen. It is knowing that God is inside of you. God will appoint you. He will make your path straight. When I encounter giants during my battles. I let my giants encounter my God through prayer. Prayer is the most power tool for spiritual warfare. I had invited God into the ring with me. Then, I put my trust in him to perform. God will justify you. It does not matter what they say. God has the final word. Remember it can't overtake you. It may slow you down but that's when God gives you divine directions and strategies to become an Overcomer.

I am a Winner! Winners never quit! Come on join me in the winner circle through FAITH!

DAY NINETEEN

1 John 2:4 AMPC

Whoever says, I know Him I perceive, recognize, understand, and am acquainted with Him but fails to keep and obey His commandments (teachings) is a liar, and the Truth of the Gospel is not in him.

Knowing God is essential in this Christian walk. Verbally acknowledging God is great, but let the world see Christ in your life. I knew that God will supply my every need. Being in the presence of God was one of the most powerful feelings, I've experienced in my life. He has allowed me to enter in his gates with thanksgiving. This experience can't be verbally express. But I know God is real. I hope that you get to a place in your life to experience his glory. You must become a doer of the word of God. Then the word will illuminate your path.

DAY TWENTY

1 Thessalonians 5:16-17 AMPC

*Be happy in your faith and rejoice and be
glad hearted continually (always); Be
unceasing in prayer praying perseveringly;*

Prayer is the key, that unlock doors. You must condition yourself to pray daily. It is your uninterrupted time in God's presence. I used this time to sit quietly and to listen to God's voice. I invite God to invade my environment. Oh boy! Sometimes, he did just that- invade my environment with his glory. He has called me by my name. That's a wonderful feeling.

DAY TWENTY-ONE

Philippians 4:6 AMP

*Do not be anxious or worried about
anything, but in everything [every
circumstance and situation] by prayer and
petition with thanksgiving, continue to make
your [specific] requests known to God.*

If I ever needed God to move on my behalf, it was in my finances. No matter how many times I did my checks and balances; There was always more month than money. But one day I heard a message by Pastor Kenneth Hagin, known as the "The Father of Faith." He spoke on this scripture and he gave four principles. He said as Christians we need to focus on God's word and follow God's principle for finances. Now, I get it. I started focusing my attention on the word of God. The word of God talks about becoming anxious so, why go against God? Think about it! Did my anxiousness improve my situation? (Matthew 6:27)

As Christian, we cannot operate like the world system. God made a promise to supply all of our needs. I have seen God do it again and again. God will provide for his children. His provisions are not wrapped in a beautiful gift box. But God does come on time. Use the WOR LD System!

DAY TWENTY-TWO

Psalm 27:14 NLT

Wait patiently for the LORD. Be brave and courageous. Yes, wait patiently for the LORD.

This is hard. Waiting on the Lord timing is HARD. Especially, when you are doing things your way. The word "Wait" in my dictionary means, it is okay to go ahead and do it. It's like telling a 1 year old to stop don't do that, they smile at you and do it anyway. That's me! I knew I had to wait on the lord, but I thought my input would help me skip or get the results faster. Oh boy, I was wrong! God timing is critical to your purpose. His timing will be aligned to your assignment. Take it from me "Wait". It will pay off, if you wait on GOD.

DAY TWENTY-THREE

Isaiah 54:2 NLT

"Enlarge your house; build an addition.
Spread out your home and spare no expense!

I don't know about you, but again this scripture was yelling at me. As I was starting my ministry, the Lord kept me focus. I was able to use my imagination to visualize the steps God directed me to take. To me this meant that God was not a territorial God. He chooses whomever he wanted to carry the gospel of Jesus Christ. (2 Corn. 3:5) His plans included opportunities beyond my zip codes and resources not linked to my bank account. I had to attached myself to the word of God, if I wanted to enlarge my territory.

DAY TWENTY-FOUR

Psalm 63:4 NLT

I will praise you as long as I live, lifting up
my hands to you in prayer.

How wonderful it is to praise his name. All I have ever known is to praise God. I wanted to be that a person who's pleasing to God. God has spared my life in many situations. I've had some near-death situations, BUT God kept his arms around me and did not let me go. For this reason, I will praise him all the days of my life. Hallelujah, he has been good to me.

DAY TWENTY-FIVE

Isaiah 43:11 NLT

> *I, yes, I, am the LORD, and there is no other*
> *Savior.*

God is it. He is the one True God. The one Supreme God over all nation. Believe this within you. Establish a relationship with the True God within you. I made God my everything. Yes, God will establish you. There's no other SAVIOR!

DAY TWENTY-SIX

Psalm 34:19 NLT

The righteous person faces many troubles,
but the LORD comes to the rescue each time.

S top worrying! God will bring you out. Trust God when you can't trace him. Know that he is there. When things got rough! This scripture leap into my spirit. He is the great. "I AM". I was tried get out of myself trouble (bad decisions) through my own efforts. I could not do it alone. BUT, when I decided to trust in God, he brought me out of those bad situations every time. He will never leave you nor forsake you. Won't He Do!

DAY TWENTY-SEVEN

Philippians 4:8 NLT

And now, dear brothers and sisters, one final thing. Fix your thoughts on what is true, and honorable, and right, and pure, and lovely, and admirable. Think about things that are excellent and worthy of praise.

This thought process unlocks the doors of happiness in your life. What you think about is, what you will become. To attract what you want you must change your mind-set, change your thought patterns. Change your self-conscious mind. Think on things that Jesus did to satisfy his father. It said to FIX your thoughts on Good things that deserve praise. My challenge to you is to change your thought process. Unblock your mind, turn your mental key and to get the results you deserve.

DAY TWENTY-EIGHT

Hebrews 11:1 GNT

To have faith is to be sure of the things we hope for, to be certain of the things we cannot see.

Oh, this scripture on faith means

F – aith

A – ctivate

V - ictories

O – f

R - ewards

F aith is hope. Hope is to be certain and your certainty can not always be seen.

DAY TWENTY-NINE

Proverbs 23:7 KJV

⁷ For as he thinketh in his heart, so is he:

You are what you think. So, what do you think about yourself? How do you see You? One of my previous sermons was title "Will the real you, please stand up?" You must clear your mind. Love you first. Encourage yourself and be the Best You! You deserve the very best. My mother said show me your friends and I will show you your future. Think about you. James Earl Jones, said " a mind is a terrible thing to waste." You can't share your big dreams with a small-minded dreamer, believer.

DAY THIRTY

Psalm 34:8

Taste and see that the Lord is good. Oh, the joys of those who take refuge in him!

───────────────❖───────────────

Wow God is so amazing. He changed ME! I changed my daily confession. I stop making excuses and began to explore God's unlimited possibilities. I got God on my side. Once I realize that he resides in ME, there was no stopping me. I was able to draw on the canvas of my imagination everything that God promise Me. God will give you the desires of your heart. IT's my Season. Join me!

www.ingramcontent.com/pod-product-compliance
Lightning Source LLC
Chambersburg PA
CBHW021946040426
42448CB00008B/1265